Did You

WHITBY

A MISCELLANY

Compiled by Julia Skinner

With particular reference to the work of Cordelia Stamp,
Robert Preedy and Maureen Anderson

THE FRANCIS FRITH COLLECTION

www.francisfrith.com

First published in the United Kingdom in 2010 by The Francis Frith Collection®

This edition published exclusively for Identity Books in 2012 ISBN 978-1-84589-516-7

Text and Design copyright The Francis Frith Collection®
Photographs copyright The Francis Frith Collection® except where indicated.

The Frith® photographs and the Frith® logo are reproduced under licence from
Heritage Photographic Resources Ltd, the owners of the Frith® archive and trademarks.
'The Francis Frith Collection', 'Francis Frith' and 'Frith' are registered trademarks of
Heritage Photographic Resources Ltd.

British Library Cataloguing in Publication Data

Did You Know? Whitby - A Miscellany
Compiled by Julia Skinner
With particular reference to the work of Cordelia Stamp, Robert Preedy and Maureen Anderson

The Francis Frith Collection
Oakley Business Park,
Wylye Road, Dinton,
Wiltshire SP3 5EU
Tel: +44 (0) 1722 716 376
Email: info@francisfrith.co.uk
www.francisfrith.com

Printed and bound in Malaysia
Contains material sourced from responsibly managed forests

Front Cover: **WHITBY, ARGUMENTS YARD 1913** 66290p

The colour-tinting is for illustrative purposes only, and is not intended to be historically accurate

CONTENTS

INTRODUCTION

It was at Whitby Abbey in the seventh century that St Hilda founded one of the most famous monasteries of the Anglo-Saxon world. St Hilda's abbey was later destroyed by Viking raiders, and the ruins we see today are of the abbey that replaced it, most of which date back to the 13th and 14th centuries. Together with St Mary's Church, the abbey ruins stand on the hill overlooking Whitby's harbour – dating back to Roman times, this is the only natural harbour between the Humber and the Tees, and so it is an important shipping haven. For many years it was easier for people coming to or going from Whitby to make their journey by sea rather than attempt to travel overland.

Situated in a deep ravine on the estuary of the River Esk, Whitby earned its living in the past from the sea, either by whaling (whaling ships once departed from here to sail to Greenland and the Arctic in search of a catch), fishing, coastal trading or shipbuilding. The fishing trade developed gradually, from the Middle Ages onwards, and in the 19th century Whitby's prosperity was particularly derived from herring fishery – large seasonal catches of this fish could be made along this coast. However, nowadays the herring fishery is all but gone, and the town relies mainly on tourism.

Many famous names in history are linked with Whitby, such as Caedmon, known to history as the first recorded English Christian poet, the two William Scoresbys (father and son), Captain Cook, the seafarer and navigator, and Bram Stoker, author of 'Dracula'. The town's story is full of fascinating characters and events, of which this book can only provide a brief glimpse.

WHITBY, BAXTERGATE 1923 74309

YORKSHIRE WORDS AND PHRASES

'Mebbe' - maybe, perhaps.

'Beck' - a stream.

'Ginnel' - an alleyway between houses.

'Gang' - to go.

'Gradely' - good, as in **'It were reet gradely'** - it was really good.

'Growler' - pork pie.

'Goodies' - sweets.

'Keks' - trousers.

'Lake' or 'laik' - to play, or skive off work, as in **'Is he laiking agin?'.**

'Lop' - a flea.

'Mytherin' - to worry about something, or as in a child being annoying - **'Stop mythering me!'.**

'Sen' - self, as in **'Get thee-sen on'** - go away.

'A bunch a'fives' - a fist, or a punch.

'Allus at't last push up' - always at the last moment.

'Brass-necked' - very confident.

'If tha' dances wi' devil, thal' ge't pricked wi'-is 'orn' - If you dance with the devil you'll get pricked by his horns, ie you will suffer if you do evil deeds.

'I'll go t'foot of our stairs!' - I'm very surprised!

'Think on' - think about it.

'It caps owt' - it beats everything.

HAUNTED WHITBY

The Bagdale Hall Hotel is said to be the oldest building in Whitby, dating from 1516. The corridors of the hall are reputed to be haunted by the ghost of a former owner, Captain Browne Bushell, who was executed for treason in 1651.

Legend says that a phantom coach and horses drives up Greenlane, thunders past the church and then plunges over the cliffs into the sea.

The byways of Whitby are supposed by some to be haunted – or more accurately plagued – by a mischievous spirit called Hob, who changes signposts round and sometimes causes motorists to skid.

A headless phantom is said to walk between Prospect Hill and Ruswarp, carrying its severed head under its arm.

When Bram Stoker, author of 'Dracula', was staying in the town he noted that 'there is a legend that a white lady is seen in one of the windows' of the ruins of Whitby Abbey. The 'ghost' was believed to be that of St Hilda, the founder of the abbey, and was referred to as 'Lady Hilda' by the local people. At one time crowds used to gather at the west side of the parish churchyard in the mid-morning, to watch for the ghost, which appeared as a shrouded figure in the highest window of the north side of the abbey; it is believed that the illusion was caused by the sun shining on the window at a certain time and angle.

WHITBY, THE PARISH CHURCH FROM THE ABBEY 1913 66279

WHITBY MISCELLANY

In Anglo-Saxon times, before this area was settled by the Danes (or Vikings), Whitby lay in the Anglo-Saxon kingdom of Northumbria. Its famous abbey was founded during this period, in AD657, by a Northumbrian princess called Hilda – later to be St Hilda – who was its first abbess. St Hilda founded the abbey for King Oswy of Northumbria in thanksgiving following his victory over the heathen King Penda of the Anglo-Saxon kingdom of Mercia.

WHITBY ABBEY 1901 46790

Most of our knowledge about the early days of Whitby's abbey comes from the writings of the monk known to history as the Venerable Bede, later St Bede. He was a monk and scholar at the monastery of Jarrow in the eighth century, and wrote one of the first history books, 'The Ecclesiastical History of the English People'. It is from him that we learn how St Hilda came to Whitby from Hartlepool in the mid seventh century and founded the monastery whose fame spread far and wide. St Hilda's abbey became a renowned centre of learning, but was probably destroyed by Vikings who raided Whitby in AD870; the ruins which can be seen today date from medieval times, when the abbey was rebuilt.

In AD644 an important ecclesiastical meeting was held at Whitby Abbey, known as the Synod of Whitby. The meeting was held to decide whether the Christian people of Northumbria should follow the teachings of the Celtic or Roman Churches, and Oswy, King of Northumbria, listened to arguments from both sides. St Colman spoke for the cause of the Celtic Church, but St Wilfrid (of Ripon and Hexham) spoke for the Roman Church, and his argument won the day. King Oswy decreed that the practices of the Celtic Church which had been introduced by St Aidan several decades earlier should be abandoned; henceforth the Roman practices would be followed, and Roman Catholicism became the primary religion of northern England until the Reformation of the 16th century.

The Caedmon Cross (see photograph 46783, opposite) was erected at the top of the 199 steps in 1898 to commemorate Caedmon, one of the most famous people from the earliest days of Whitby Abbey. Its Celtic design shows the figures of Christ, David, Abbess Hilda and Caedmon himself. Caedmon was an illiterate cattle herder who worked at the abbey, and legend says that he would hide in a cow shed when others around him began to sing, embarrassed because he was unable to hold a tune himself. One evening he fell asleep whilst he was hiding, and dreamt that an angel came to him and taught him how to sing. When he awoke he found that he had dreamed a true vision and now had a wonderful gift for singing, and used his new-found talent to tell of the creation and God's world in song. When Abbess Hilda heard of his talent she took him into the monastic community and he became a monk. Hilda encouraged him to use his gift to spread the word of God. The Venerable Bede, in his 'The Ecclesiastical History of the English Nation' (AD731), tells Caedmon's story: 'There was in the Monastery of this Abbess a certain brother particularly remarkable for the Grace of God, who was wont to make religious verses, so that whatever was interpreted to him out of scripture, he soon after put the same into poetical expressions of much sweetness and humility in English, which was his native language. By his verse, the minds of many were often excited to despise the world, and to aspire to heaven'. Bede records the song of Creation which Caedmon sang for the angel, and later for Abbess Hilda:

'Praise we the Fashioner now of Heaven's fabric,
The majesty of his might and his mind's wisdom,
Work of the world warden, worker of all wonders,
How he the Lord of Glory everlasting,
Wrought first for the race of men Heaven as a rooftree,
Then made he Middle Earth to be their mansion.'

WHITBY
THE CAEDMON CROSS
1901 46783

**WHITBY
ABBEY ARCHES
1913** 66281

After the mid eighth century the abbey at Whitby disappeared from the historical record for some time, and was probably destroyed by Viking raiders around AD870. It was not until the 11th century that the stone abbey which is familiar to us today was begun by Norman Benedictine monks during the revival of monasticism in England, and it became a monastery for men. The abbey was altered and rebuilt over the years; most of what we see today dates from the 13th and early 14th centuries. Then the greed and rapacity of Henry VIII brought about the end of the monasteries, and Whitby Abbey was dissolved in 1539.

Photograph 66281 (opposite), taken in 1913, shows a very different picture of the abbey ruins from today's carefully mown and tended lawns. After the lead had been removed from the abbey's roof after the Dissolution it was not long before the structure began to crumble, and much of the abbey's building stone was taken away for re-use elsewhere – a few monastic stones can be found around the town in some Whitby walls and buildings. The west front largely collapsed in 1914 during the First World War after a raid by German battle cruisers, which shelled Whitby and scored a direct hit on the abbey. The façade has since been partially rebuilt.

Whitby was formerly in the old North Riding of Yorkshire, one of the three historic subdivisions of the county (alongside East and West Riding) which were abolished in 1974; most of North Riding was then replaced by the new non-metropolitan county of North Yorkshire. It was the Viking Danes who settled in Yorkshire who first divided the huge county into the 'ridings'. Originally, they were 'thridings' – or thirds – and they became the North, East and West Ridings. That ancient Danish and Norse heritage is still evident today in many Yorkshire place-names, especially in place-names ending in 'by' like Whitby – 'by' is the Viking word for 'town'.

In medieval times the town of Whitby was a snug collection of small houses clinging to the cliffs below the abbey; they were arranged in numerous yards, each of which was enclosed by a sturdy gate strong enough to repel any seaward invasion.

In former times Tin Ghaut (seen in photograph 66292, opposite) was one of many narrow alleyways leading down to the harbour area. 'Ghaut' is a Viking word for a narrow passage leading to the river. There used to be an inn at the end of this one, so in the local dialect it became known as T'inn Ghaut. Tin Ghaut was just off Grape Lane, once home to the Yorkshire-born explorer Captain James Cook, who is remembered in monuments and museums all around the north-east coast. The charming view seen in the photograph no longer exists, as Tin Ghaut was demolished in 1959 to make way for a car park.

Whitby has always been a busy trading port. In the 16th century, locally mined alum was the main cargo, and in the 16th and 17th centuries coal was shipped to and from Tyneside. In the early 18th century Whitby was the sixth most important port in England. Trading still continues nowadays – Whitby imports and exports timber, limestone, paper and steel products.

Whitby also developed a shipbuilding industry, and at one time around 130 ships a year were built here. The town developed a reputation for building ships which were exceptionally durable and strong, and the shipyards were famous for their quality of construction. They were particularly known for their collier-barks, also known as 'cats' – these were sturdy, three-masted sailing ships designed for the coastal coal-carrying trade between Newcastle and London, which had flat keels to allow cargoes to be easily loaded and unloaded, often from the beach. Large cargo vessels continued to be built in the shipyards until 1908. Today, fishing boats, mainly Yorkshire cobles, are still built at two small boatyards. A coble (pronounced 'cobble') is a very ancient type of fishing boat that goes back to Viking times. It is clinker built, with a flat bottom for landing on the beach.

WHITBY, ARGUMENTS YARD 1913 66290

Photograph 66290 (opposite) shows Argument's Yard in Church Street, one of the many narrow yards running down to the river near the harbour, which at the time of this photograph were occupied by fishermen and poorer families. Argument's Yard is named not as a result of a quarrel but after a family that once owned property there. Although this location was a favourite subject for artists and photographers, life was very hard for the inhabitants, these barefoot boys amongst them. Providing boots and shoes for the children was a major problem for parents, and there was a special local charity for this purpose to assist them.

Whaling was once a major part of Whitby's economy. Between 1766 and 1816, the Whitby whaling fleet's catch included 2,761 whales and around 25,000 seals, and blubber warehouses were erected along the inner harbour, where the smelly business of rendering the blubber into oil took place. Whale oil was very important in the past, and was used for lamp oil, lubrication, and in the manufacture of soap, textiles, varnish, paint and explosives. The great days of whaling lasted from about 1735 to the early years of the 19th century, but the loss of the whaling ships 'Lively' and 'Esk' in 1826 heralded the end of the whaling boom.

One of Whitby's most famous landmarks, and a reminder of the importance of whaling to the town in the past, is the arch on West Cliff made from a pair of whale jaw bones, close to the Captain Cook monument. During the whaling years, when a ship was returning to Whitby's harbour from a whaling trip it was the custom to trice up a pair of whale jaw bones to the mast, decorated with ribbons, as a sign that the voyage had been successful and the ship was full.

In medieval times there were hardly any roads to Whitby except for a few narrow, stony tracks over the moors; almost all access to the town was from the sea. A bridge was a late innovation, built in the 16th century – before then, the river had to be crossed by fords. This bridge was a wooden drawbridge, rather Dutch in style; it was rebuilt in 1766, and demolished in 1835, to be replaced by a stone bridge. The present swing bridge dates from 1908, and the high level bridge further up river was opened in 1980 to allow traffic to bypass the town. In photograph 46788 (below) we can see the swivel-section of the stone bridge, built in 1835 to replace the old Dutch-style drawbridge, open to let a ship through. Then, as now, crowds have gathered to watch the operation.

WHITBY, THE BRIDGE 1901 46788

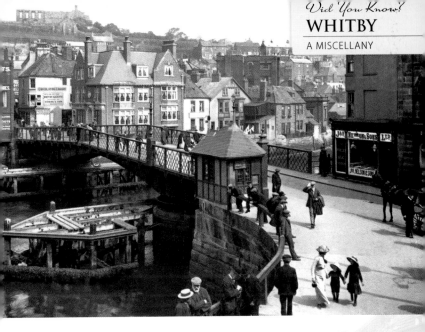

WHITBY, THE BRIDGE 1913 66266

The new bridge, which was completed in 1908, was welcomed by pedestrians and ships alike (see photograph 66266, above). Its two sections span 75 feet; each action can be operated independently, swinging horizontally. The bridge is electrically operated. It is manned for two hours on either side of high water, and vessels request opening by radio.

In photograph 66263 (below) we are looking towards the East Cliff, where the old St Mary's Parish Church and the ruins of Whitby Abbey stand. St Mary's Church is 12th-century, consisting of a nave, chancel and tower. Though the exterior is plain, the interior is one of the most outstanding in England. There are galleries on every side; box pews date back to the 17th century; there is a three-decker pulpit of 1778; and all is lit by candlelight. The church was made famous by Bram Stoker in his Gothic novel 'Dracula' as the place where the count sought refuge in the grave of a suicide.

WHITBY, EAST CLIFF 1913 66263

Adjacent to the abbey ruins is St Mary's Parish Church, which is reached from the harbour by a flight of 199 steps known as 'Jacob's Ladder' (photograph 66284, below). It is thought that the church steps were originally built in the early 14th century to enable access to the church from the old town, and at that time the steps were wooden, not stone. The steps we see today are about 200 years old, and were probably built by local and itinerant labourers. In former years coffins would have been carried from the town below all the way up to the church for funerals, and there are still 'coffin rests' to be seen here.

WHITBY, CHURCH STAIRS ('JACOB'S LADDER') 1913 66284

On the right of photograph W81040 (below) is St Michael's Church, which was demolished in the 1960s. Directly above the church is Abbey House, the one-time home of the Cholmley family; Richard Cholmley, 'the great black knight of the north', leased and later bought Whitby Abbey after the Dissolution. His son Francis remodelled the old abbot's lodging and used it as his house. Sir Hugh Cholmley improved Abbey House in the 1630s and his son, also Hugh, built an impressive classical-style range in front of the older building in 1672 – unfortunately it fell into decay after the loss of its roof in the 1790s. In 1866 the house was again extended by W C Strickland. It was later run by the Co-operative Holiday Association as a holiday hotel. A new Visitor Centre was constructed inside the restored Cholmley range in 2002.

WHITBY, THE UPPER HARBOUR c1955 W81040

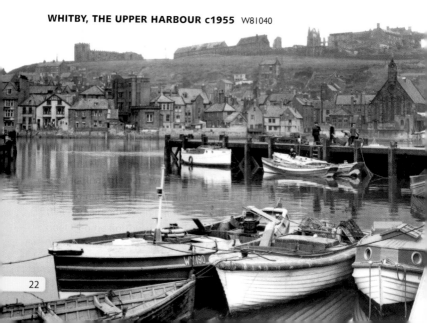

WHITBY, THE PARISH CHURCH, GALLERY ENTRANCE 1913 66287

In photograph 66287 (above) the churchwarden awaits the arrival of the owners of the abbey (who at this date would have been the Stricklands), ready to escort them up to their private gallery in the parish church; the gallery was built in the early 17th century by the Cholmleys, who had owned the abbey since the Dissolution. The churchwarden stands by the Huntrods' tomb, which commemorates Francis and Mary Huntrod – they were both born on 19th September 1600, married each other on their birthday, and both died on their birthday in 1680, within five hours of each other.

Photograph 18190 (below) shows the ancient village of Sandsend, nestling in the shelter of Lythe Bank. Many of the men who worked in the alum industry and on local estates lived here. Alum was a chemical used in tanning leather and in the dyeworks to fix the dye used in the weaving industry. It was mined and extracted from local stone in the Whitby district, both at Sandsend and Saltwick, and provided much work for the miners. It became obsolete with the introduction of other chemicals. Today, many of the dwellings in Sandstone are holiday cottages.

Captain James Cook the famous navigator, surveyor and sea captain, came to Whitby at the age of seventeen, where he was apprenticed to John and Henry Walker, local ship-owners. Cook's first experience as a sailor was in 1747, when he embarked from Whitby on the 'Freelove', a coal carrier. He spent some years in the coasting and Baltic trade, and then joined the Navy, where he rose through the ranks, becoming master in 1759. He displayed exceptional ability as a navigator and surveyor, and in 1768, after surveying the St Lawrence River in Canada and the Newfoundland coast, he commanded the 'Endeavour' for the Royal Society expedition to the Pacific, Australia and New Zealand. This was the first of his three major expeditions, in each of which he sailed in boats built in Whitby, including the 'Endeavour' and the 'Resolution'. He also worked out how to prevent his crew suffering from scurvy on long sea voyages. A statue of Captain Cook overlooks Whitby harbour from West Cliff. Designed by John Tweed, the statue was presented to the town of Whitby by Gervase Beckett MP in 1912. Cook has a map in one hand and dividers in the other and, as the sculptor intended, he looks out to sea, his eyes on the distant horizon.

WHITBY
CAPTAIN COOK'S MONUMENT
1913 66270

Did You Know?
WHITBY
A MISCELLANY

The panoramic view of Henrietta Street and East Cliff shown in photograph 74310 (below) was probably taken from the West Pier extension. The lighthouse there was built in 1831 from the design of Francis Pickernell, the engineer to the harbour trustees; it is worked manually, and is used only when vessels are expected. Its green light has a range of ten miles. It is 83 feet tall, and is open to the public – there is a fine view from the top. The smaller lighthouse on the East Pier (54 feet tall) was erected in 1854. The lighthouses were essential to guide ships safely to harbour, as this rocky coast has claimed many victims.

Whitby harbour was renowned for its narrow entry between the two piers with their lighthouses. The whaling ships had to wait for high tides to carry them through safely. The little fishing cobles had not problems, provided the wind was in the right quarter.

WHITBY, EAST CLIFF 1923 74310

Whitby has had numerous lifeboats. Among many heroic rescue attempts, perhaps the most tragic was in 1861, when only one of the lifeboat crew, Henry Freeman, escaped death because he was wearing a newly-invented cork lifejacket.

Whitby expanded rapidly in the Georgian period, the town's wealth developing from the expansion of the shipping trade, both in the whaling trade and maritime commerce. Shopkeepers and tradesmen were quick to take advantage of the boom, and 52 grocers and 30 drapers are listed by George Young, the famous historian, in his 'History of Whitby' in 1817. He also lists numerous masons and bricklayers, glaziers, hatters and hairdressers, ship chandlers and victuallers. At this time, he tells us, the town contained 7 jewellers' shops, 6 hardware shops, 6 toy shops and 6 slop shops (a slop shop sold ready-made clothes); dealers in ale and porter amount to 65 and in tea 72, but it appears that the 83 dealers in tobacco exceed the others.

WHITBY, EAST CLIFF 1932 85342x

Drying the washing was always a problem for housewives in the past. In photograph 85342x (opposite) we can see that it is washday, and that someone has pegged out her linen on a line on Tate Hill sands. Old deeds of many of the East Cliff houses often included particulars of 'drying ground', the rights of which came with the building in question. The concerned housewives of settled the problem between themselves as to which days 'their' portion of the drying ground might be available – and then presumably prayed for a fine day!

Two famous names in Whitby's history are those of a father and son, both named William Scoresby. William Scoresby senior was born in 1760 south of Whitby. He was apprenticed to a Whitby ship owner and served on whaling ships. He rapidly worked his way up to command a Greenland whaler, the 'Henrietta', in 1790, and the 'Dundee' in 1798, and was remarkably successful, catching 80 whales between 1792 and 1797. He formed a partnership to build a new Greenland whaler, 'Resolution', launched in 1803; in 1810 he formed the Greenock Whale and Fishing Company with three Greenock businessmen. His whaling exploits were finally ended when his ship 'Fame' was destroyed by fire in the Orkneys. His retirement years were devoted to improvements for Whitby, including suggestions for lengthening the pier. He died in 1829. One of his other claims to fame is that he invented the 'Crow's Nest' used on ships as a look-out. The Crow's Nest was made of wood and canvas, not metal as this would adversely affect the ship's compass, and was large enough to contain a man, a telescope and a shotgun.

William Scoresby junior's fame rests on his achievements as an explorer and scientist. Born in 1789, he served as a boy on his father's whaling ships, then went to Edinburgh University, where he studied chemistry and physics. After a spell in command of his father's whaler the 'Resolution', he commanded the 'Esk', in which he explored Arctic seas and lands and carried out experiments on the temperature of the sea. In 1806 the two Scoresbys attained a Furthest North record, reaching 81°30 north, the nearest approach to the North Pole ever made by sailing ship. In 1820 William Scoresby junior published 'An Account of the Arctic Regions', the first scientific account of the area, and in 1822 he surveyed 400 miles of the Greenland coast. In 1825 he was ordained to the Church, but he continued with his scientific investigations. In 1838 he was asked by the Admiralty to assist with the construction of compass needles. Shortly before his death in 1857 he sailed to Australia to study terrestrial magnetism.

Photograph 18170 (below) shows Larpool Viaduct, which was originally erected for the Scarborough and Whiby Railway. The first brick was laid in 1882 and the first locomotive crossed the thirteen-arched viaduct in 1884. Trains from Scarborough crossed the viaduct, stopped at West Cliff and then reversed steeply down beneath the viaduct into Whitby.

The coming of the railway in the 19th century changed Whitby. It was now firmly on the map, and its narrow crowded alleys, its ruined abbey and its souvenirs made from jet (fossilised wood found in the local area) proved a magnet for day trippers and holiday-makers. The holiday trade led to the development of the town, chiefly in the direction of the West Cliff, where hotels and guest houses were built.

WHITBY, THE VIADUCT 1884 18170

WHITBY, ROYAL CRESCENT 1923 74307

As Victorian Whitby developed as a resort, 19th-century property developers put up more and more boarding houses to accommodate the new influx. Chief among these was George Hudson, 'the railway king'. Born in Yorkshire in 1800, he used a legacy to buy railway shares, which started his career of investing in the railways and forming railway companies. At the height of his success in the early 1840s he and his companies controlled over a thousand miles of railway track, and he had amassed a considerable fortune. He dominated the greater part of Whitby's West Cliff with his property development schemes, and intended to surpass Bath and its famous crescents with his own Royal Crescent development in Whitby. Sadly, both George Hudson's fame and his money ran out before the crescent could be completed and fulfil his dream of out-doing Bath. Today we only see half of his original ambitious design, shown in photograph 74307 (above).

The author Bram Stoker stayed at Number 6, Royal Crescent in 1890, and the house in which he lodged is seen in the centre of photograph 74307 (above), behind the lamp post; it was here that he started to write his most famous book, 'Dracula', setting much of it in Whitby.

Did You Know?
WHITBY
A MISCELLANY

In the year in which photograph 18168 (below) was taken, 1885, Whitby was poised for a summer influx of new visitors via the new Scarborough to Whitby Railway, which opened on 6th July 1885. Down in the harbour, the tall ship seen in this view was moored just in front of the Angel Vaults, still here as a waterside inn. In between the tall houses on the far right of the harbour was Tin Ghaut, seen in photograph 66292 on page 15.

WHITBY, THE HARBOUR 1885 18168

WHITBY, FROM BOGHALL c1886 18165

The view shown in photograph 18165 (above) demonstrates clearly that the River Esk is tidal, for it shows vessels lying on the river bed at low tide. The houses on the left of the photograph were built after the advent of the railway in the 1830s and although they were named Fishburn Park, in honour of the local ship-building family, they are known locally as 'The Railway'.

Some of the photographs in The Francis Frith Collection were supplied to Francis Frith's company by the Whitby photographer Frank Sutcliffe. He was born in Leeds in 1853, and set up his professional photographic studio in Waterloo Yard, Whitby, in 1875 before moving to premises in Skinner Street. From the 1880s he made photographic studies of the vanishing world of the farm workers and particularly the fishermen of Yorkshire. From the late 1890s he used the new lightweight cameras, and so was able to capture spontaneous moments.

If the railway viaduct (see page 32) is a memorial to its bricklayers, then how much more should the two piers at the harbour mouth be a tribute to the engineers and masons who first built them. They knew their job, for they built them to withstand the tremendous force of storm winds and tides – and still they stand. It is uncertain how old the piers are, but the first mention of them is in Henry VIII's time. There was great rejoicing when the new stone and iron extensions were finally erected in 1912, having first been suggested by William Scoresby the elder (1760-1829) a hundred years before. The extensions effectively enlarged the harbour entrance, making it safer for vessels to enter harbour in rough weather. The competent engineers left a space for turbulent seas to break through and lessen the strain on the masonry. The pier extensions were constructed with the aid of a 'walking man', a huge metal scaffolding contraption that moved along the seabed to enable the building process. A foghorn on the west extension gives a blast every thirty seconds when visibility is poor.

WHITBY, THE NEW PIER EXTENSIONS 1913 66265a

WHITBY, FISH QUAY 1923 74318

Whitby's fishing trade developed gradually. From the Middle Ages onwards the prosperity of the town was largely derived from fishing; large seasonal catches of herring could be made along the coast, and during the 19th century Whitby became an important herring centre. In photograph 74318 (above) we see the early morning scene at the fish market after the catch has been landed and sorted. The auctioneer is at the very far end.

In past years a widespread tradition in Whitby was that the sea-going male fraternity endeavoured to invest their hard-earned savings in houses bought in their wife's name so that she would have an income should they be drowned, a not uncommon event then; this was a prudent precaution in the days before the welfare state.

By the time of photograph W81147 (below) the humble fishing
cobles had developed into a sizeable fishing fleet of much larger
boats, which meant that they could travel further afield for their
catch. At the time of the herring fleet's arrival from Scotland
(following the seasonal migration of the herring shoals), the fishing
boats completely filled the harbour, and it used to be said that one
could walk right across the river without using the bridge, by walking
across the boats.

WHITBY, SAILING FROM THE HARBOUR c1955 W81147

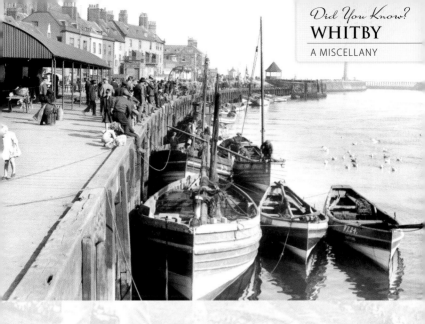

WHITBY, THE QUAY 1927 80177

Photograph 80177 (above) shows Whitby's old fish market on the left. Years ago the quay would have been bustling with women gutting the herrings and packing them into barrels with salt and ice. Visitors still come here today to look at the catches brought in by the Whitby trawlers, but the local fleet nowadays is a tiny one in comparison with the fleet of 100 years ago. A new fish market exists on this site now, but little else is changed, and the lighthouse on the new pier still guides ships back into the shelter of this welcoming harbour.

Photograph 28862 (below) was taken by the Whitby photographer
Frank Sutcliffe, and as its original title shows, the children in this view
were indeed twins, but were actually boys. They have recently been
identified as Matthew (left) and Robert Peart, three years old when
this was taken. In later years Robert's life was tragically cut short
when he drowned after being swept overboard near St Petersburg
on 19th July 1908, aged 20, and his younger brother George (the
baby being held by his sister Amelia in photograph 28866, opposite)
also died by drowning, aged 23, when the HMS 'Hogue' was sunk
during the First World War, on 22nd September 1914.

WHITBY, 'GEMINI' 1891 28862

WHITBY, THE PEART CHILDREN 1891 28866

Photograph 28866 (above) is another view taken by Frank Sutcliffe and is a study of the local Peart children; their parents were Jane (née Leadley) and David Peart, and the family lived on Tate Hill. In this photograph the Pearts' eldest daughter Amelia (17) holds her baby brother George; Amelia later married Tom Eglon. The twin boys (Matthew and Robert) take a rather damp seat on the seaweedy rock, and Jane (nicknamed Ginny) and Tom watch the photographer put them all in the frame for posterity. Jane (Ginny) married Ernest Swales, a ship's carpenter, in 1909. She died in 1977 at the grand old age of 92 years. She bore three daughters and four boys, and also stillborn twins, giving birth to her youngest child at 44 years old. There were also two other brothers in the family who are not shown in this photograph, David and William Peart. There are several descendants of the Peart children still living in the Whitby area, and we are grateful to everyone who has contacted The Francis Frith Collection with information, helping us to identify them.

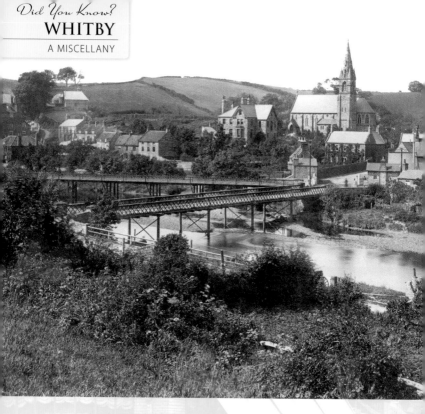

RUSWARP, THE BRIDGE c1881 14491

Old documents relating to Whitby refer to the western part of the town as Ruswarp, although the village itself lies about a mile from the town. Photograph 14491 (above) shows the old road bridge, which was washed away in disastrous floods in the 1920s; the railway bridge is to its left.

In 1923, when photograph 74297 (below) was taken, Whitby could boast no less than five hotels in the Dunlop Motorist's Guide: The Angel (telephone number Whitby 57), The Royal (with 172 bedrooms and garage parking for 20 cars), The Metropole, The Custom House and the 70-bedroom West Cliff. The Metropole Hotel (seen in the photograph) was one of the first in Whitby to have electric light, and its glowing windows were used by ships as a landmark.

Whitby owes much to Queen Victoria, who went into permanent mourning after the death of her husband, Prince Albert, in 1861; all was black thereafter, as she made the outward show of sorrow fashionable, and the town's jet industry came into its own. Craftsmen appeared all over Whitby working on jewellery and other items made from jet, a hard, black material which is actually fossilised wood from Araucaria trees. It was fortunate that around twenty million years ago there must have been a forest of these trees around the Whitby area, for Whitby's is one of the best deposits of jet anywhere in the world. Local men were not slow to start digging up the black gold all along the coastal area. Jet lends itself to intricate carving and a high polish, and a local man, Captain Tremlett, invented a way of turning jet to make beads. Jet trinkets soon became highly desirable, and in the 1870s about 1400 men and boys were employed in the industry. However, by the 1930s demand had decreased and the industry dwindled drastically, although it is still possible to buy jet jewellery in Whitby shops today. There are some wonderful examples of the jet craftsmen's skills in Whitby Museum.

WHITBY, WEST CLIFF AND THE METROPOLE HOTEL 1923 74297

The main method of recruitment for the Royal Navy in the Georgian period, and especially during the Napoleonic Wars, was impressment – the seizing of men between the ages of 18 and 55 by press gangs stationed around the coast; press gangs also took men coming ashore from warships or snatched them from merchant ships on the high seas. Although whaling crews were supposed to be exempt from impressments, as whale oil was in such high demand, this was not always observed and the proviso was sometimes lifted by the government. Ports like Whitby were prime targets for the press gangs, and Whitby men were particularly sought after for their seafaring skills. Impressment was often a violent process, both in the way that the press gangs abducted potential recruits and in opposition from the local population of the ports and harbours frequented by the gangs. There was much to fight for, as if a man was taken his family could be left in poverty. On 26 February 1793 a serious riot occurred in Whitby when the sailors of the town rose up against the press gang, drove them out of town and destroyed their 'rendezvous', or 'safe house', in Haggersgate. A letter to an officer at the Admiralty from Lieutenant Atkinson, RN, Keeper of the 'Whitby Rendezvous', described how the press gang's meeting-place was attacked by a mob of about a thousand men and women: 'The women supplied the men with large stones and bricks; the windows of the house were instantly demolished, but the resistance of the Gang kept them out till nine, when with Capston bars they broke the door to pieces and rushed in, as many as the House and yard could contain; they turned the Gang out, and treated them in the most savage and cruel manner, some of them nearly murdered; the furniture of the House destroyed and carried off, the landlord almost killed, and the actions of this banditti was of the most horrid nature.' An old man who was seen encouraging the sailors was subsequently tried, condemned, and executed at York as one of the ringleaders of the riot; a woman called Hannah Hobbs was also tried and transported for life for aiding the rioters.

The 19th-century novelist Mrs Elizabeth Gaskell stayed in Whitby with her daughters and heard about the Whitby riot. She found out as much as she could about the event by talking to local people, and used the story as the background for her tragic novel 'Sylvia's Lovers', published in 1863; set during the Napoleonic Wars, the book gives a vivid picture of a press gang attacking home-coming sailors in Monkshaven (Whitby) who have landed from Greenland.

Demolition took its toll on what we can see on the left side of this photograph. On the opposite side we can still identify the corner building and the Friends Meeting House, and between them is one of the oldest houses in Whitby, certainly Tudor and possibly much older. In the 16th century its roof was thatched.

WHITBY, CHURCH STREET 1925 78982

SPORTING WHITBY

Whitby Regatta takes place every year over three days in August, and is believed to be the oldest sea regatta in England. The event has now expanded to include other attractions such as a funfair and firework display, but was originally held as a local rowing competition between local fishermen in their boats. It later became a major event for yacht racing, but nowadays rowing has once again become the major part of the event.

Rivalry at Whitby Regatta is intense between three old-established local rowing clubs – the Whitby Friendship Amateur Rowing Club, the Whitby Fisherman's Amateur Rowing Club and the Scarborough Amateur Rowing Club. The most important trophy competed for at the Regatta is the 'Wilson Cup', open to rowing clubs based between the Tyne and the Humber.

Whitby Town Football Club is one of the oldest clubs from Yorkshire's North Riding, formed by an amalgamation in 1926 of two local teams, Whitby Whitehall Swifts and Whitby Town, which had changed its name from Streaneshalch FC a year after its founding in 1880. The new club was originally called Whitby United, but became Whitby Town in 1949.

In the 1990s Whitby Town FC had a great run, winning the Northern Premier League First Division, the Northern League Cup six times, and the FA Vase (in 1996–97). Another notable season was 2004/05, when Whitby Town equalled an earlier club record of playing 19 games without being defeated.

WHITBY, THE STEPS TO THE CHURCH
c1955 W81045

DUKE OF YORK

Did You Know?
WHITBY
A MISCELLANY

QUIZ QUESTIONS

Answers on page 52.

1. What was the Anglo-Saxon name for the town of Whitby?

2. What is the nickname of Whitby Town Football Club?

3. What place in Whitby's history is held by Henry de Vall?

4. Who is Pannett Park named after?

5. Khyber Pass (see photograph 66271, opposite) is the name given to the road up from the beach in Whitby – but where in the world is the more famous Khyber Pass that this road is named after?

6. What is the name of the river that empties into the North Sea at Whitby?

7. The famous explorer, navigator and explorer Captain Cook began his maritime career when in the 1740s he was taken on as a merchant navy apprentice by John and Henry Walker, prominent Whitby ship-owners, in their small fleet of vessels plying coal along the English coast; the Walkers' house in Grape Lane is now the Captain Cook Memorial Museum. The Captain Cook Monument is a prominent local landmark on West Cliff, overlooking Whitby harbour, but where in the world did Captain Cook meet his death?

8. What – to modern eyes – was unusual about the monastery/abbey which St Hilda founded in Whitby in AD657?

9. Whitby is famous for its deposits of jet, from which jewellery and other items are made. Jet is formed from the fossilised remains of Araucaria trees – by what name are these trees better known nowadays?

10. How did events in Whitby in ancient times give us the expression 'a moveable feast'?

RECIPE

STUFFED HERRINGS WITH MUSTARD SAUCE

Herrings were a particularly important catch for local fishermen in the 19th century. The use of mustard with herrings is said to have been a culinary tradition introduced by the Vikings, who settled this area over a thousand years ago, and is a favourite accompaniment to herrings in many parts of north-east England.

4 large herrings
3 heaped tablespoonfuls fresh
    white breadcrumbs
1 heaped teaspoonful finely
    chopped parsley
A squeeze of lemon juice
Grated rind of half a lemon
Salt and black pepper
Oil for frying
25g/1oz butter

Mustard Sauce
40g/1½ oz butter
25g/1oz plain flour
450ml/ ¾ pint milk
Salt and black pepper
1 level tablespoonful dry
    mustard powder
1 tablespoonful wine vinegar
1 level teaspoonful caster sugar
Lemon wedges and fresh
parsley sprigs for garnish

Remove the heads from the herrings, clean, gut and bone them. Wash the herrings and pat them thoroughly dry. Put the breadcrumbs, parsley, lemon juice and lemon rind in a basin; season lightly with salt and freshly ground black pepper. Melt the butter and stir into the breadcrumbs to bind the mixture, which should now be moist, but crumbly. Stuff the herrings with the breadcrumb mixture, and if necessary secure them with wooden cocktail sticks. Slash the skins crossways two or three times on each side; brush the herrings with oil and wrap each in foil. Put the herrings in a well-buttered deep baking dish; cover with lightly buttered greaseproof paper and bake in the centre of a pre-heated oven at 200°C/400°F/Gas Mark 6 for 35-40 minutes.

For the mustard sauce, melt 25g/1oz of the butter in a pan; stir in the flour and cook for 1 minute. Gradually stir in the milk, beating well until the sauce is quite smooth. Bring to the boil and simmer for 2-3 minutes; season with salt and pepper. Blend the mustard powder with the vinegar and stir into the sauce; add the sugar. Check seasoning and stir in the remaining butter. Transfer the baked herrings to a hot serving dish and garnish with wedges of lemon and sprigs of parsley. Serve the mustard sauce separately.

RECIPE

YORKSHIRE CURD TART

The distinguishing and traditional characteristic of Yorkshire Curd Tart is allspice (or 'clove pepper' as it was also known) but this may not be to modern tastes, so mixed spice can be substituted for the ground allspice if preferred.

For the pastry:

115g/4oz butter, diced

225g/8oz plain flour

1 egg yolk

For the filling:

A large pinch of ground allspice, or mixed spice if preferred

90g/3½ oz sugar

3 eggs, beaten

Grated rind and juice of 1 lemon

40g/1½ oz melted butter

450g/1 lb curd cheese, or cottage cheese if curd cheese is hard to find

75g/3oz raisins or sultanas

To make the pastry: rub the butter into the flour until the mixture resembles fine breadcrumbs. Stir the egg yolk into the flour mixture with a little water to bind the dough together. Turn the dough on to a lightly floured surface, knead lightly and form into a ball. Roll out the pastry thinly and use to line a 20cm (8 inch) fluted loose-bottomed flan tin. Chill for 15 minutes.

To make the filling: mix the ground allspice or mixed spice with the sugar, then stir in the eggs, lemon rind and juice, melted butter, curd or cottage cheese and dried fruit. Pour the filling into the chilled pastry case, then bake in a pre-heated oven (190°C/375°F/Gas Mark 5) for about 40 minutes until the pastry is cooked and the filling is lightly set and golden brown. Serve still slightly warm, cut into wedges with cream.

QUIZ ANSWERS

1. The Anglo-Saxon name for Whitby was 'Streonshalh'. The name is remembered in the Streonshalh area of the town. In later years the Danes, or Vikings, who settled in this area named their town 'Hviteby', which means 'The White Town'.

2. Whitby Town FC are known as 'The Seasiders'.

3. Henry de Vall was the last abbot of Whitby Abbey. He was forced to surrender the abbey to Henry VIII's commissioners in December 1539, during the Dissolution of the Monasteries.

4. Pannett Park is named after Alderman Robert Elliott Pannett who bought the Chubb Hill Estate to give to the town, and arranged for it to become a public park in his will of 1917. Formerly this area was an orchard and market garden, and a few fruit trees from those days can still be found in the park.

5. Khyber Pass in Whitby, cut through solid rock and connecting West Cliff to the harbour, is named after the strategic pass between Afghanistan and Pakistan which was the scene of several battles fought by British forces in the Afghan Wars of the 19th century.

6. The River Esk. The river flows through the town and divides it into two parts. The older part of the town is on the East Cliff, under the abbey. The West Cliff area of the town was developed in the 19th century.

7. Captain Cook's last voyage was to discover a passage round the north coast of America from the Pacific, but he was forced to turn back in the Bering Strait, reaching Hawaii in 1779. Here he was attacked and killed by natives, at the age of fifty.

8. The early Anglo-Saxon monastery at Whitby Abbey which was founded by St Hilda in AD657 was a double monastery for both men and women. The monks and nuns were segregated and lived in separate communities, but worshipped together in the church.

9. Araucaria is a type of what is popularly known as the Monkey Puzzle tree.

10. It was at Whitby Abbey in AD664 that the Synod of Whitby was held to resolve the differences between Celtic and Roman Christianity, particularly over calculating the date of Easter, the most important holy festival in the Christian Church. Following the synod, the English Church was unified under the Roman discipline, and the date of Easter Day was settled as the first Sunday after the Paschal full moon. Because Easter itself is a holy day whose date is not fixed to a particular day of the calendar year, the dates of all the other Christian festivals – or 'feasts' – which are linked to it are also changeable, in response to the date of Easter for that year, and thus are known as 'moveable feasts'. Easter itself can also be called a 'moveable feast'.

WHITBY, NEW QUAY ROAD 1936 87334

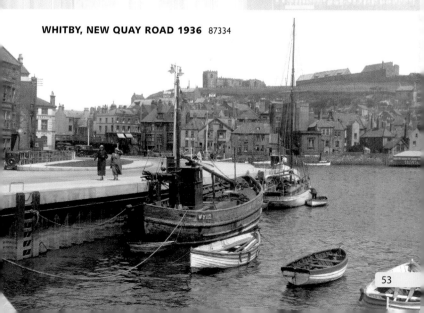

FRANCIS FRITH

PIONEER VICTORIAN PHOTOGRAPHER

Francis Frith, founder of the world-famous photographic archive, was a complex and multi-talented man. A devout Quaker and a highly successful Victorian businessman, he was philosophical by nature and pioneering in outlook. By 1855 he had already established a wholesale grocery business in Liverpool, and sold it for the astonishing sum of £200,000, which is the equivalent today of over £15,000,000. Now in his thirties, and captivated by the new science of photography, Frith set out on a series of pioneering journeys up the Nile and to the Near East.

INTRIGUE AND EXPLORATION

He was the first photographer to venture beyond the sixth cataract of the Nile. Africa was still the mysterious 'Dark Continent', and Stanley and Livingstone's historic meeting was a decade into the future. The conditions for picture taking confound belief. He laboured for hours in his wicker dark-room in the sweltering heat of the desert, while the volatile chemicals fizzed dangerously in their trays. Back in London he exhibited his photographs and was 'rapturously cheered' by members of the Royal Society. His reputation as a photographer was made overnight.

VENTURE OF A LIFE-TIME

By the 1870s the railways had threaded their way across the country, and Bank Holidays and half-day Saturdays had been made obligatory by Act of Parliament. All of a sudden the working man and his family were able to enjoy days out, take holidays, and see a little more of the world.

With typical business acumen, Francis Frith foresaw that these new tourists would enjoy having souvenirs to commemorate their days out. For the next thirty years he travelled the country by train and by pony and trap, producing fine photographs of seaside resorts and beauty spots that were keenly bought by millions of Victorians. These prints were painstakingly pasted into family albums and pored over during the dark nights of winter, rekindling precious memories of summer excursions. Frith's studio was soon supplying retail shops all over the country, and by 1890 F Frith & Co had become the greatest specialist photographic publishing company in the world, with over 2,000 sales outlets, and pioneered the picture postcard.

FRANCIS FRITH'S LEGACY

Francis Frith had died in 1898 at his villa in Cannes, his great project still growing. By 1970 the archive he created contained over a third of a million pictures showing 7,000 British towns and villages.

Frith's legacy to us today is of immense significance and value, for the magnificent archive of evocative photographs he created provides a unique record of change in the cities, towns and villages throughout Britain over a century and more. Frith and his fellow studio photographers revisited locations many times down the years to update their views, compiling for us an enthralling and colourful pageant of British life and character.

We are fortunate that Frith was dedicated to recording the minutiae of everyday life. For it is this sheer wealth of visual data, the painstaking chronicle of changes in dress, transport, street layouts, buildings, housing and landscape that captivates us so much today, offering us a powerful link with the past and with the lives of our ancestors.

Computers have now made it possible for Frith's many thousands of images to be accessed almost instantly. The archive offers every one of us an opportunity to examine the places where we and our families have lived and worked down the years. Its images, depicting our shared past, are now bringing pleasure and enlightenment to millions around the world a century and more after his death.

For further information visit: www.francisfrith.com

INTERIOR DECORATION

Frith's photographs can be seen framed and as giant wall murals in thousands of pubs, restaurants, hotels, banks, retail stores and other public buildings throughout Britain. These provide interesting and attractive décor, generating strong local interest and acting as a powerful reminder of gentler days in our increasingly busy and frenetic world.

FRITH PRODUCTS

All Frith photographs are available as prints and posters in a variety of different sizes and styles. In the UK we also offer a range of other gift and stationery products illustrated with Frith photographs, although many of these are not available for delivery outside the UK – see our web site for more information on the products available for delivery in your country.

THE INTERNET

Over 100,000 photographs of Britain can be viewed and purchased on the Frith web site. The web site also includes memories and reminiscences contributed by our customers, who have personal knowledge of localities and of the people and properties depicted in Frith photographs. If you wish to learn more about a specific town or village you may find these reminiscences fascinating to browse. Why not add your own comments if you think they would be of interest to others? See **www.francisfrith.com**

PLEASE HELP US BRING FRITH'S PHOTOGRAPHS TO LIFE

Our authors do their best to recount the history of the places they write about. They give insights into how particular towns and villages developed, they describe the architecture of streets and buildings, and they discuss the lives of famous people who lived there. But however knowledgeable our authors are, the story they tell is necessarily incomplete.

Frith's photographs are so much more than plain historical documents. They are living proofs of the flow of human life down the generations. They show real people at real moments in history; and each of those people is the son or daughter of someone, the brother or sister, aunt or uncle, grandfather or grandmother of someone else. All of them lived, worked and played in the streets depicted in Frith's photographs.

We would be grateful if you would give us your insights into the places shown in our photographs: the streets and buildings, the shops, businesses and industries. Post your memories of life in those streets on the Frith website: what it was like growing up there, who ran the local shop and what shopping was like years ago; if your workplace is shown tell us about your working day and what the building is used for now. Read other visitors' memories and reconnect with your shared local history and heritage. With your help more and more Frith photographs can be brought to life, and vital memories preserved for posterity, and for the benefit of historians in the future.

Wherever possible, we will try to include some of your comments in future editions of our books. Moreover, if you spot errors in dates, titles or other facts, please let us know, because our archive records are not always completely accurate—they rely on 140 years of human endeavour and hand-compiled records. You can email us using the contact form on the website.

Thank you!

For further information, trade, or author enquiries please contact us at the address below:

The Francis Frith Collection, Oakley Business Park, Wylye Road, Dinton, Wiltshire SP3 5EU.
Tel: +44 (0)1722 716 376 Fax: +44 (0)1722 716 881
e-mail: sales@francisfrith.co.uk **www.francisfrith.com**